Little Book of Instant Fun with Grandkids

These projects are recommended for children 8 and above. Grandparents, always carefully supervise your grandchildren when enjoying these activities together, especially around water, in the kitchen, or when using sharp objects. Remember that any activity involving small parts can present a choking hazard and is not suitable for children under the age of 3. Before beginning any activity, take into consideration your grandchildren's ages, abilities, and any allergies they may have, and adapt your plans accordingly. Stay safe and have fun!

Grandma's heart is a
patchwork of love.

Little Book of Instant Fun with Grandkids
ISBN 978-1-7350245-3-0
Published by Product Concept Mfg., Inc.,
2175 N. Academy Circle #7, Colorado Springs, CO 80909
©2020 Product Concept Mfg., Inc. All rights reserved.
Written and Compiled by Vicki Kuyper in association with
Product Concept Mfg., Inc.

You're an Awesome Grandma!

Let's face it, even the most awesome grandma can use a helping hand now and then. This little book of instant fun can turn a trip to grandma's house into a treasure trove of happy memories. Geared for ages 8 and up, each activity, craft, and game, can easily be tweaked to suit the age and interest of your own unique grandkids. Peruse it before they arrive. Keep it in your purse when you're on the go. Or let your grandkids thumb through it and choose their new favorite way to spend the day. Just add a little imagination and a whole lotta love!

Nature Wristband

The next time you go on a walk with your grandkids, encourage them to bring some of the Great Outdoors back home with them. Before you head out, fashion a clear packing tape or duct tape "wristband" around their wrist—sticky side out. Then, head outside! Encourage your grandkids to pick up feathers, flowers, leaves, seeds... whatever catches their fancy, and attach them to their bracelet in a decorative way.

Colorful Scavenger Hunt

A scavenger hunt at Grandma's house
is a game that's stood the test of time.
Try a twist on this old favorite by
having your grandchildren close their
eyes and choose a crayon from your
hand. Then, have them search your
house for items that are the same
color as the crayon they chose.
Hand them each a piece of paper
or notepad and a pencil. Ask them to
list each item of their color by name
and the room where they found it,
leaving the item in place.

Mix-Up Cups

Using clear plastic cups and washable markers, your grandchildren can create a mix-up of different people. On the first cup, have your grandchildren draw legs and shoes in the lower third of the cup. On the second, a torso and clothing in the middle third of the cup. On a third, a face in the top third of the cup. Then, have them stack the cups to create a person. Have your grandchildren swap cups to make different people. Try this with different animal parts, as well, to create a crazy new species.

Fire-Breathing Dragon Craft

Gear up for a dragon battle by helping your grandchildren make their own fantastical beasts—that even breathe imaginary fire! All you need are empty toilet paper tubes, colored crepe paper, tape, and crayons or markers. Cut 4" to 6" strips from a roll of crepe paper. (Red, orange and yellow are the most "fire" authentic colors, but any color will do. After all, this is a mythical beast!) Cut slits about ¼" to ½" wide up from the bottom of each piece of crepe paper, keeping a 1" rim intact at the top of each strip. Tape this rim onto the inside of toilet paper roll. Color the rest of the dragon's head onto the roll. When grandkids blow through the back end of the roll, the dragon will "breathe" fire.

Hit-the-Hole
Sponge Toss

Your grandchildren don't need a
special board to play the game.
Simply draw chalk circles on your
driveway or patio to serve as
targets. You can add different
numerical amounts below the
targets, if they want to play for
points. Substitute wet sponges for
beanbags. (This will help them stay
in place when they land.) Then,
let the tossing tournament begin!

Walking Water

Grandkids observe how water
travels up ... though celery!
Place a stalk of celery in a
glass of water mixed with
food coloring, and watch with
your grandkids as the colored
water makes its way up the stalk.
Best of all, colored celery
is great to eat.

Bottle Bowling

Turn a hardwood or linoleum floor into Grandma's Bowling Alley. Line up 10 plastic water or soda bottles. Put four in the back row, three in row three, two in row two, and one in the front row—forming a triangular formation. Use a small, indoor ball for your "bowling" ball. You can also take this idea to the garage or sidewalk, and instead of a ball, use a rolled up sock.

Car and Kid Wash

If the weather is hot, and you don't happen to have a pool, your grandchildren can still have a splashing good time. Have them don swimsuits and wash your car. If you have a dedicated car wash product to use, that's great.

If not, water, clean rags or sponges, and a fair amount of elbow grease are all your grandkids really need. Prepare yourself for some happy smiles, a moderately clean vehicle, and plenty of wet and wild shenanigans by the time they're through.

Flapjack Relay

Here's a way to enjoy breakfast
without having any dishes to wash. Cut
circles out of cardboard or use small plastic
storage container lids. Make as many stacks
of "flapjacks" as you have grandchildren.
Place each stack on a table at one end of
the room. On the opposite end of the room,
place a plate for each stack. When you say
GO, each grandchild has to maneuver one
pancake onto their spatula (no extra helping
hands allowed!) then hurry across the room
and deposit it on their plate. When their plate
is full, each grandchild has to hurry back
to the starting point, carrying their plate
in one hand and their spatula in the other.
Whoever gets their flapjack-filled plate back
on the table first, wins.

Single Sentence Story Time

Build a story together, one sentence at a time! Choose who will begin the story. Only one sentence allowed! Each person takes a turn adding a single sentence to the ongoing narrative. Continue until you feel the story is complete—or you're finished waiting in line!

It was the last day of school.

I had big plans for a fun summer.

But suddenly, everything changed...

Fort Fantasy

Building a fort out of blankets, pillows, carboard boxes, etc., is a time-honored childhood tradition. Enjoy a twist on tradition by helping your grandchildren design a fort that fits a specific theme, such as a pirate ship, an airplane, a castle, a race car, a spaceship... whatever invites their imaginations to take flight!

Who Will I Be?

Invite your grandchildren to draw themselves—as adults. What do they think they will look like and what will they do? Will they draw an astronaut, a teacher, a ballet dancer, a firefighter, or...? They can include in the scene the vehicle they might drive, or the home they live in. You might want to try this activity every year and see how much their drawings, and their dreams, evolve over time.

Thankfulness
in Every Day

Help your grandchildren become
more aware of all they have to
be thankful for by incorporating
reasons for gratitude into games
and crafts. Have them draw
a picture that includes 10
different things they are
thankful for. While riding in the
car or waiting in line, take turns
voicing something each person is
grateful for. Challenge them to
see who can make the longest
list of things they appreciate.

Rock Out

Have your grandchildren make a colorful addition to your patio or garden with original rock art. Begin by gathering rocks with a flat surface. Clean them with a bit of dish soap and water and allow them to thoroughly dry. Your grandchildren can use acrylic paints, permanent markers, or even nail polish to create their desired design. To help maintain a cohesive design, give your grandchildren a set theme, such as, abstract designs, bugs, funny faces, colorful letters spelling out things they are thankful for, or different elements of a fairy village. When their artwork is complete coat it with a safe spray sealer. If you don't happen to have any on hand, you can also use a coat of clear nail polish.

Creepy Critters

Challenge your grandkids to draw creepy critters from simple shapes. Have them draw a triangle—then have each one create an insect incorporating the shape they've drawn. Continue suggesting other shapes, seeing how many insects they can come up with, both real and imagined.

Act Out!

Here's a variation of an
old favorite that takes no
preparation, just imagination!
Have each grandchild take turns
"acting out!" For example, try
imitating an animal—without
making any sounds! See how
long it takes to guess what their
chosen critter happens to be.
Try other subjects, such as
occupations (act out what a
teacher would do, a farmer, pilot,
or plumber) or Bible stories
(act out David and Goliath,
Noah's Ark, Daniel in the Lion's
Den, the Nativity story).

Mystery Picture

All you need for this game is a piece of paper and a pencil, marker, or crayon for each participant. Have one grandchild stand facing a wall, holding a piece of blank paper up against it. Then, have another grandchild stand behind him or her, placing their piece of paper on their sibling's back. Have that child begin to draw a picture. The grandchild facing the wall has to try and replicate the drawing he or she feels being drawn on their back. The end result is bound to be laughter-worthy.

Freeze Frame Dance Party

Although your taste in music may not always line up with that of your grandchildren, here's a way you can introduce them to your favorite songs, share a few laughs, AND help them burn off a little energy indoors. Turn on your favorite CD or radio station. Keep the remote in hand. Begin with something fast and upbeat. Ask the kids to dance or move to the music in any way they like. When you hit the pause button, have everyone freeze in place. See who's in the craziest pose. Feel free to join in the fun! Ask your grandkids to bring their favorite music with them on their next visit (or ask your voice-controlled personal assistant to play their favorite tunes!). It's a great way to get a little exercise while getting to know each other better at the same time.

Who Are You?

What do your grandchildren know about you—other than the fact that you're an awesome grandmother? Try playing 20 Questions: The Family Version. Have your grandchildren ask you any question they'd like, such as, "How old are you?" "Where did you go to school?" or "What was your favorite toy when you were a kid?" To help get the ball rolling, ask your grandkids questions, such as, "What do you like best about your best friend?" "What's one thing you'd like to learn how to do?" or "What do you like best about coming to my house?" Knowing how to ask "getting to know you better" questions is a helpful relational skill, regardless of your age. Why not begin a tradition of asking one question about each other during every meal you share together?

Big Foot Sneakers

Take two empty, standard-sized tissue boxes. If you like, have your grandkids decorate them with markers or stickers. Set up an easy obstacle course of pillows and chairs that "Big Foot" has to walk around or jump over. Have your grandkids take turns donning the Big Foot sneakers and running the obstacle course, while you time them on your phone. (Layer pairs of socks on their feet to make the cardboard sneakers fit well enough to not fall off as they run.) Depending on the age of your grandkids, they can also simply wear them around the house, imagining what it would be like if Big Foot actually visited Grandma!

Nutty Bird Feeder

Take empty toilet paper tubes and have your grandchildren spread a thin layer of peanut butter over them. Place bird seed in a pie tin or plastic food storage container. Have your grandchildren roll the peanut butter covered cardboard tubes in the bird seed until they are covered. (The tubes...not the grandkids!) Then, have your grandchildren hang their bird feeders by sliding each tube onto a different tree branch. Talk about which kind of bird each one of you thinks will show up first—then watch from a distance to see who flies in to feast!

Journey to a New World

Create a new country! (Your grandkids can each make up their own country or you can brainstorm ideas together as a team.) Figure out whether it will be located in this world, on a planet somewhere in space, or in a totally fictional locale. Come up with a name, what its inhabitants will look like, local clothing styles, what they'll use for currency, etc. Draw a map of this new world, noting important sites. Create stamps and a flag. Write its history. Make up a travel guide, including a few phrases in the local language and a menu of national dishes. This activity can be one you can continue working on together for years to come!

Break the Rules

Sometimes, breaking unwritten rules is not only a good thing, but can make a memorable day for grandkids and grandmothers alike. Make today the day! Serve breakfast for lunch or dinner. Wear pajamas all day. Turn the bathtub into a reading nook for a grandkid—just add pillows, blankets, and pull the curtain for privacy! (The one thing not to add is water!) Let your grandkids have an indoor camping trip where they sleep under the kitchen table (easily turned into a tent by covering it with a large blanket), equipped with flashlights, sleeping bags, and microwaved s'mores. The list of unwritten rules you can enjoy breaking together is as expansive as your imagination!

Fairy Feast from Down Under

Although Fairy Bread isn't well known outside of Australia and New Zealand, there's no reason why it shouldn't become one of your grandkids' favorite treats. Simply spread a slice of white bread with butter. Cut off the crusts and slice the bread into triangles. Sprinkle a layer of colorful nonpareils generously over top. Then, enjoy! Although nonpareils means "having no equal" in French, if you don't happen to have the little round rainbow-colored cookie decorating staple, any type of decorative sprinkles (including jimmies, quins, dragées, or sugar pearls!) can be used. To make the treat extra festive, try cutting the bread with a cookie cutter.

Indoor Ice Rink

When it's too cold, or too hot, to play outside, you can easily turn any clean hardwood or linoleum floor into an ice arena. All you need are dryer sheets and barefoot grandkids. Set two unused dryer sheets on the floor for each grandkid. Then have your grandkids put their bare feet directly on top, one for each foot. The dryer sheets will stick to their feet enough to make an impromptu pair of skates. (If you don't have dryer sheets, you can also use a large pair of fuzzy mittens, if you don't mind that they may get stretched out of shape after a day of play!) Turn on some skating tunes and let the fun begin!

Cup Catch

Give each grandchild a large plastic
cup. Have them try to toss an object
back and forth to each other,
using only the cup in their hand.
Try a squishy, small rolled sock, tiny
plastic toy, fresh cherry, grape, or
blueberry...use your imagination!
Have them try tossing and catching
objects of different weights, sizes,
and shapes—and move farther apart
from each other as they master
each different object.

Coloring Book Remake

If you have coloring books your grand-children have outgrown, but that still have unused pages, repurpose them into a color-by-number challenge. Beginning with "1," write sequential numbers into every white space on the coloring page, using the same number for spaces that would likely be the same color. Along the top of the page, list the numbers and draw a small box below it. Let your grandkids decide what color to pair with each number—and color the corresponding box with a crayon, marker, or colored pencil. Then, watch your grandkids create a new kind of masterpiece.

It's a Bird, It's a Plane...
It's My Grandkids!

Help bring out the champion in your grandkids by making them their very own super-hero cape. It's as easy as 1, 2, 3! 1. Find a well-worn, crew neck tee shirt that you no longer use, one that's ready for the donation bag. 2. Using scissors, cut the front part of the shirt (including the shoulder seam, sleeves, and side seam) away from the elasticized neck, leaving the ribbed neckband intact. 3. Stretch the neckband over your grandchild's head and let their imagination soar! (If you have the resources on hand, encourage your grandkids to decorate their capes with fabric markers.)

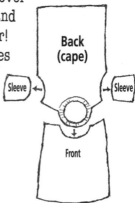

Back
(cape)

Sleeve ←   → Sleeve

Front

hello

Learn a New Language

You don't have to speak to learn a new language! Learn some basic words in American Sign Language together. Choose simple words you will use frequently, such as, Love, Grandma, Family, Cat, Dog, Brother, Sister, and Thank You. You and your grandkids can even make up a few of your own, creating silent, secret messages you can communicate to one another without speaking a word.

I Love You

goodbye

Blindfolded Builder

If you're like most grandparents, you probably have a stash of interlocking plastic blocks on hand. Make building more challenging by giving each grandchild a pile of blocks—and then blindfold them with a bandana or dish towel. Have your grandchildren build different objects simply by touch... a house, a car, an airplane, etc.

Frosty Caterpillar Sundaes

Any grandma can scoop ice cream into a bowl. Go above and beyond by treating your grandkids to an ice cream caterpillar sundae. Line up several small scoops of ice cream (use a cookie dough scoop to limit the size of the scoops) on a plate. Let your grandkids decorate their caterpillar treats with sprinkles, small candies, raisins, fruit gummies…whatever you have on hand. Don't forget the pretzel stick antennae!

Suitcase Dress-Up Race

In between vacations, why not put your luggage to work? Fill two suitcases or carry-ons with several pieces of clothing, making certain each case contains the same number of items. (Warning: these items may get stretched out or even a bit torn. Choose carefully!) Pack a variety...pants, hats, belts, socks, scarves, handbags, shoes, etc. Using your phone as a timer, have your grandkids compete against each other as they put on every item in their suitcase. Only one grandchild? This is your chance to get in on the fun! Exchange suitcases and try again. Next, put on the clothing, take it all off, hand it to the other team, and then do the same with their clothing. Up for another challenge? Try it blindfolded!

British Party Crackers

Is there a birthday, special event, or holiday on the family calendar? Make British party crackers with your grandchildren to use at the celebration. You'll need as many empty toilet paper tubes as there will be guests at the party, as well as wrapping paper, tape, ribbon, and "prizes" or candies. Place a small handful of candy and/or prizes into each tube. Add a hand-written fortune, if you like. Carefully roll the gift wrap around the tube. Tape it in place. Leave about 2 inches of paper extending from either open end. Gently twist the gift wrap on each end. Tape around the twist to hold it in place. Tie a piece of ribbon over the tape. At the party, have guests pull open the end of their cracker to reveal their surprises.

Sock-It-To-Me Carnival Toss

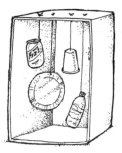

Tie strings of different lengths from the pull-tab on several soda cans. (You can also poke a hole in the bottom of a disposable cup and lace a string through it, securing it with a large knot.) Tie several of these hanging "targets" from a bathroom shower curtain rod. You can also set a large cardboard box on its side and secure the targets inside the top of the box with masking or shipping tape, so they hang freely at different lengths. Have each grandkid stand at a set distance from the targets and see how many they can hit with a balled-up sock. The better they get, the farther they have to move away from the target.

"To Dye For" Dinners

Make any meal more fun with a
little bit of food coloring! For a
simple pasta dish, fill as many
pots with water as you have
grandchildren. Have each grandchild
add their choice of dye to their own
personal pot. Boil, then drain, the
pasta. Top each plate of individually
colored pasta with a small amount of
olive oil and salt, or butter. Set out
bowls containing different kinds of
shredded cheese, small pieces
of ham, chicken, or salami,
cooked peas, broccoli florets,
or mushrooms—and have your
grandkids top off their dish
in their own special way.

Create a Reading Nook

Encourage your grandchildren to fall in love with a good book, by creating a special place just for reading. It could be a closet, the corner behind a chair in the living room, a crawlspace under the stairs, a makeshift tent in the backyard, or a temporary indoor fort built from blankets, pillows, and chairs. Lend them a flashlight, or set up a camping lantern, if it adds to the ambiance. Create a "kids' shelf" on an existing bookcase and add new and used titles to it as finances allow. You can also set a good example, by scheduling a designated "reading time" when they visit. Don't forget to join them in taking time out to read a good book— and to share your reviews of the books you're reading with one another.

Snowball Relay

Any season is the perfect time for a snowball race. All you need are cotton balls, teaspoons, and some energetic grandkids! Place a bowl of cotton balls on a table and two empty bowls (one for each team—even if that's just you and one granchild) across the room. Make the game more difficult by setting the bowls somewhere else in the house—preferably up a flight of stairs! Begin by having a member of each team maneuver a single cotton ball onto their teaspoon (without using their hands) and then carry it to their team's empty bowl. After placing their cotton ball in the bowl, they hurry back to the starting line to repeat the process until all of the cotton balls are gone. The team with the most cotton balls in their bowl wins.

Stack It High

This is a simple activity that can be adapted to almost any item you happen to have on hand. Grandchildren can compete against each other, against you, or against themselves. The goal is to see how many of any of one item you can stack before the "tower" falls over. Try pennies, books, disposable cups, bars of soap, magazines, granola bars, canned goods, decorative pillows...the list is only as limited as your imagination! Or try mixing a variety of items to build the tallest tower possible.

The Family Gazette

Turn your dining room into a newsroom by helping your grandchildren create a family newspaper. Depending on how "high tech" you and your grandchildren want to go, stories can be handwritten on large sheets of paper or typed onto a computer, formatted, and printed for the enjoyment of the whole family. Brainstorm a name for the paper, design a masthead, and talk about what family stories are newsworthy, including accomplishments, holiday hijinks, vacations, funny stories, family pet antics, etc. As time and interest allow, add family recipes, original cartoons, photos, opinion pieces, book reviews, and Want Ads. Who knows? The creation of an annual edition could become a family tradition—and cherished keepsake.

On Point Art Project

George Seurat became famous with his paintings composed of nothing but dots. You can unleash the budding pointillist painter in your grandchildren, using nothing but paper, paint (watercolor, acrylic, children's washable paints—anything you may have on hand), and cotton swabs. First, share some examples of pointillism from any art books you may have in your personal library or search for references online. Chat with your grandchildren about different styles of art, decide on a subject to paint, then grab a cotton swab and begin. Use a clean swab for each color of paint. You can also use fine point felt tip markers, if you prefer.

Rainy Day Rambunctiousness

If the weather is inclement, but your grandchildren could use some "outside" play time, pull the car out of the garage, carport, or driveway. Let your grandkids use that extra space to roller skate, jump rope, play on their skateboard or bike, bounce a ball, play tag or put on music and have a dance party. (Be sure to move any sharp or toxic items to a safe place first.) Having the opportunity to make a bit more noise, and move around a little more freely, can help them burn off some of their excess energy and keep everyone's mood more upbeat.

Index Card Architect

An index card is more than just a convenient place to jot down recipes. It can also be a compact, economical building block used to construct a miniature city. All it takes is a bit of patience, a steady hand, a little folding, and an active imagination. Help your grandchildren try folding a stack of index cards in different ways. (If they've been used, all the better! Here's a clever way to reuse them!) Next, challenge your grandchildren to build a structure using both flat and folded cards. See who can build the tallest building! And the next time you're headed to a restaurant, put a package of index cards in your purse. While you're waiting for your order, your grandkids can be happily occupied building a city that's easy to put away once the food arrives.

Two Truths and a Lie

A "play it anywhere" game (that's also a great "getting to know you better" tool) is "Two Truths and a Lie." Everyone takes a turn making three statements about themselves, two of which are true. One is a total fabrication. The other players try to guess which of the three statements is the lie. Your grandchildren will be amazed to learn some truths about you, particularly about what you and your life were like before they became a part of it.

Squishy Sculptures

Miniature marshmallows and toothpicks are all the building materials your
grandchildren need to construct animals,
buildings, bridges, vehicles,
and people. Why not invite
them to use the dining
room table to build
an entire squishy village?

ReWrite

Here's an anytime,
anywhere game that only requires
imagination to play. Choose a
book or movie everyone is familiar
with. Each person gets the chance
to rewrite the story. Change a
character, where the story takes
place, what era the story is set in,
etc. You can either work
together as a team (adding to
each other's changes) or each
person can create his or her
individual take on the original.

Roll It Up!

Transform cookie dough into a unique treat, using any of your favorite home-made recipes or pre-made slice-and-bake dough. Brainstorm with your grandkids about what might make a tasty outer coating that would complement the cookie. Form the dough into small balls. Then, roll each ball in your choice of topping. Try crushing graham crackers, potato chips, breakfast cereal, or hard candy. A topping of chopped nuts, crispy bacon pieces, sesame seeds, and even spicy tortilla chips can all add some extra zing to your favorite recipe. (Bake according to the original recipe.) Be adventurous! See what flavors you love and if there are any you consider a "flavor fail." You may just create a new family favorite!

Share the Love

Short and sweet, "Share the Love" is an impromptu game that could easily become a family tradition. Everyone takes a turn telling each other one thing they like, or love, about each other. Keep it going! Play this in the car, standing in line, or sitting in a waiting room. It's a "game" that you'll hope becomes a habit.

Animal Antics

It's estimated over 80% of the plants and animals in this world have yet to be discovered. Today can be the day your grandkids create a new species of their own! All you need is a piece of paper and a pen or pencil. One grandchild begins by making one line on the paper, with the end goal of creating a new animal. The next participant adds another line, and so on and so forth, with each grandchild (and grandma!) taking a turn adding lines until everyone agrees that the animal is "complete." Then give it a name and decide where it lives, what it eats, and what its habits are like.

I ♥ You

If you're looking for something to keep your grandchildren occupied for a few minutes while you're standing in line, waiting for dinner to finish cooking, or stuck in traffic, hand them a pencil and a piece of paper or small notebook. Have them draw a heart on the paper. Then, see how many things they can create using the heart as part of the drawing. Butterflies, angels, feathers, flowers, faces... The longer the wait, the more chance they have to exercise their imagination and artistic talent.

Alphabet Safari

Have fun while reinforcing spelling skills by hosting an alphabet safari. Give each grandchild a piece of paper and a pencil. Have them write the alphabet down the left-hand side of the page. Then, have them search around your home for 26 different items, each beginning with a different letter of the alphabet. If your grandkids are stumped by the letter X, you can give them an alternative, like "find an X on a magazine or book cover".

Copy Cats

Here's a simple game you can play anywhere, anytime. Have your grandchildren try to mimic what you do. Try making a funny face, clapping out a rhythm, imitating an insect...you name it. Then, give each grandchild a turn initiating the action that will be copied. Laughter is sure to ensue!

Obstacle Course Challenge

Using string, gift wrap ribbon, or crepe paper, turn a hallway into an obstacle course. Attach your "trip wires" by tying them to door handles and spring door stops. Use masking tape or painter's tape to attach them to the wall or baseboards. Leave enough room in between the string for grandchildren to wiggle through. Challenge your grandchildren to make it through the obstacle course without touching anything. Once they've mastered the course, add "obstacles" to make it more difficult.

Backwards Break

Add a touch of silliness to your time together with a Backwards Break. Put your clothing on backwards. Wear sunglasses on the back of your head. Serve breakfast for lunch or upside-down cake for breakfast. Try reciting the alphabet backwards. Try writing your name while looking in a mirror. Eat lunch with your nondominant hand. See how many palindromes you can come up with (words or phrases that say the same thing backwards as they do forward, such as pop, mom, racecar, or "Was it a cat I saw?"). And don't forget to say "hello" when it's time for your grandkids to leave!

Snowball Fight

When temperatures soar, cool things down with an indoor snowball fight. Have each grandchild build a simple "fort" on opposite sides of the room. A dining room chair or mound of pillows works well. Give each child an equal number of wadded balls of discarded printer paper. Begin the game by saying, "On your mark, get set, SNOW!" Then, let the snowballs fly. When all teams are out of paper balls, gather them up and get ready to begin again. Celebrate a final truce with a popsicle or snow cone treat.

Paper Plate Snakes

With a paper plate and a pair of child-safe scissors, your grandchildren can create their own slithery serpents. Have each child draw a spiral line from the center of the plate outward toward the edge. The tighter the spiral, the skinnier the snake. Then, have them cut along the line they've drawn from the outside in and then cut an identical line an inch or so away. Once they've cut out their snake, they can decorate it with crayons or markers. If you have plastic "googly eyes" on hand, glue them to the head. To make a "snake mobile," help your grandkids attach a string to their snake's head, so they can make him slither up and down.

Fantastic Flower Gardens

Here's a quick-and-easy craft using cotton swabs and glue. Have your grand-children cut the swabs into two pieces, varying the sizes as they like. Create flowers by gluing the swabs onto a piece of construction paper. Add a bit of color to the "petals" by adding a few drops of food color into small bowls of water. Dip the swabs into the different colors, squeezing off the excess water, and quickly drying fingers on a paper towel. Have your grandchildren finish off their gardens any way they wish. Glue real leaves collected from outside onto each flower. Use cotton balls for flower centers or clouds in the sky. Use crayons or markers to fill in the background.

Mystery Message

Need an easy distraction to
keep the grandkids occupied for a
few minutes? Have them
write messages to each other—
with their nondominant hand.
Have another grandchild read
the message aloud. Trying to
decipher the message can be
harder than it sounds!

Who Am I?

Do you have a page of kid-friendly
stickers? That's all you need to
play Who Am I. As the emcee, you
place a sticker on the forehead
of one of your grandchildren
without them seeing what it is.
That grandchild gets to ask 20
"yes or no" questions before
guessing who or what is on his
or her head. For instance,
"Am I alive?" "Am I an animal?"
"Am I bigger than a car?"
Have a couple extra sticker sheets
to send home as prizes!

Laundry Basketball

When a traditional hoop isn't
available, try having your
grandkids shoot balled up
socks into a laundry basket.
The more adept your grandkids become at the game, the
farther you move the basket
across the room.

Photo Frames

Help your grandchildren create a special gift for Mom and Dad with CD jewel cases you're no longer using. Have your grandchildren place one of their drawings, or a photo you've taken of them, in each of four empty CD cases. The next step is your job grandma: using a hot glue gun, glue the four cases together to form a square. Allow them to dry. Then, glue one more case to the bottom of the square to form a pencil holder your grandchildren's parents will be proud to display on their desk.

Quick Pickles

Are your grandchildren pickle lovers? Teach them how to make their own with this quick and easy recipe: Slice small cucumbers into spears or coins. Pack them tightly into a clean jar. Combine 2 C of vinegar, 2 tsps. of salt, and 8 tsps. of sugar, stirring until the sugar dissolves. Pour the vinegar solution over the cucumbers to fill the jar. (If needed, make more vinegar solution or top off the jar with straight vinegar.) Screw on the lid, leaving it a little loose. Refrigerate the pickles for one to two days. Enjoy!

Are We There Yet?

Taking a road trip? Invite your grand-kids to help with the planning, giving each child their own map to mark your route. Share how many gallons of gas your car holds, how many miles you get to the gallon, and the cost of a gallon of gas. Have your grandkids figure out how much gasoline it will take to reach your destination, how much the fuel will cost, where on the route would be the best place to stop and fill up, etc. Once you're in the car, have the grandkids keep their maps close at hand, crossing off every town and landmark along the way. They'll have a much better understanding of the adventure ahead and won't continually ask, "Are we there yet?" They'll know the answer!

City Word Search

When you're on the road, challenge your grandchildren to a travel word search. Before you get in the car, give each grandchild a small notebook and pencil. (You may want to attach a pen to a spiral notebook with one end of a piece of string tied to the clip of the pen and the other to the notebook's spiral wire.) Every time you enter a town, have your grandchildren write its name at the top of a blank page of the notebook. Have them see how many new words they can make out of the letters in the town's name. When you reach your destination, see who came up with the most words along the way.

Let 'Er Rip!

Turn a well-read magazine into a masterpiece! Have your grandchildren tear blocks of color out of magazine pages and glue them together to create a landscape on a large sheet of paper. No scissors allowed! Demonstrate how to tear a circle of yellow for the sun or little green ovals to use as leaves. Show them how they can glue several torn pieces of a similar color together to make a larger shape. Challenge them to try making a specific subject, such as a bird, a house, or a person. Then, display their completed works of art with pride.

This is Me!

Help your grandchildren see themselves in a new, artistic way by making self-portraits out of unconventional materials. Have them scour your pantry, gathering items, such as dried beans, nuts, candies, and dried pasta. Then, give them a large piece of sturdy paper or cardboard and some glue. Help them figure out what could represent their eyes, lips, nose, hair, and eyebrows. Or you can forfeit the cardboard and glue and put a variety of items on the table for snack time. Have your grandchildren "draw" on their plates with fruit and veggie slices, cheese sticks, crackers, and cold cuts. Then, they get to eat their portraits!

Back to School Basics

Heading back to school in the fall is always a special event. Help your grandchildren prepare for their special day by creating personalized sneakers. All you need are fabric markers and a light-colored pair of sneakers. Use sneakers the grandkids have on hand or surprise them with a special Back to School gift of new, light-colored shoes they can decorate any way they wish. Have them sketch their ideas on paper first. Then, they can choose their favorite to execute in permanent marker.

Hidden Masterpiece

Painting with "invisible ink" can be a challenge but yields interesting results! Combine equal parts baking soda and water, mixing until the baking soda dissolves. Using a cotton swab, toothpick, or paintbrush, have your grandchildren paint a picture on a piece of white paper with the baking soda mixture. Allow it to dry for about 10 minutes. To reveal their artwork, your grandchildren can paint over the paper with balsamic vinegar or thawed grape juice concentrate, using a paintbrush or sponge. (Be careful, and cover clothes and work surfaces as these can stain clothing and carpeting.) A blow dryer, set on high, will also reveal the hidden masterpiece!

Save the Spoon!

Here's a game that takes strategy and a steady hand. Using a small carboard box, have your grandchildren make a maze of crepe paper, string, or yarn across the top. Have them leave spaces that are wide enough to get their hands through, but complex enough so that this isn't easily done. Place a spoon at the bottom of the box and have your grandchildren see who can remove it in the shortest amount of time without touching any of the "trip wires."

Continue the game with objects of different sizes and shapes. You can also use a tool such as kitchen tongs instead of hands.

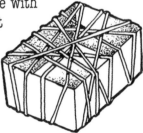

Dicey Rhymes

All you need is a single die borrowed from a board game to challenge your grandchildren to a round of rhymes. Whoever rolls the die has to come up with as many rhyming words as there are dots on the die—in 10 seconds or less. Start the timer on your phone every time a grandchild rolls a die. Once a rhyming word is used once, it can't be used again. Depending on the age of your grandchildren, and how difficult you want to make the game, try rolling a pair of dice! (You can play this by letting a child select the rhyming pairs they think of on their own, or Grandma can think of a word, (such as car or cake) and ask them to see how many rhyming words they can come up with.

Boat Float

Challenge your grandchildren to build a boat that can stay afloat while carrying 100 pennies. The one rule is that they need to ask your permission to use any of the materials they choose. They can either work together as a team or compete against one another. Try out every "seaworthy" vessel in the bathtub, a large mixing bowl filled with water, or a neighborhood creek!

Brown Bag Kite Flight

Your grandkids don't need a fancy kite
to enjoy the fun of flying one. All they
really need is a small paper bag and
string. Fold the open end of the bag back
about 1½ inches. Tape or staple a piece of
string (about 5″ long) to each corner
of the open end of the bag. Tie these
strings together into a knot. Tie a long
string (from 3′ to 5′) to the knot.
Then, all that's left to do is hold
tightly to the end of the long
string and RUN! If they
like, your grandchildren
can also decorate their
bag kites or add
a fancy tail.

Luscious Layers

Here's a mini-science lesson your grandkids can eat! Pour a small amount of Italian soda syrup or fruit-flavored pancake syrup in the bottom of a glass. Using a spoon, have your grandkids carefully pour some lemonade onto the syrup. (It's best to let the lemonade drizzle down the inside of the glass.) Add food color to carbonated water and carefully drizzle that onto the lemonade. Float a piece of fruit on top. Explain that sugar molecules contain LOTS of densely packed atoms. The less sugar, the fewer atoms, the less dense a liquid is, allowing one liquid to float on another. Drink up! Try different syrups, fruit juices, and sodas to test their density—and to decide which flavors create the tastiest combination.

Funny Face Toast

Here's a quick and easy breakfast that's bound to become a family favorite. Give your grandchildren each a piece of toast spread with nut butter or cream cheese. Then, have them turn their toast into a funny face or animal by adding fresh berries, slices of banana and strawberry, pretzels, breakfast cereal, etc. Get them started by demonstrating how to make butterfly wings with strawberry slices, sliced banana eyes with a blueberry pupil, or bubbles for a goldfish from o-shaped oat cereal.

Dessert Burgers

Your grandchildren will enjoy making this snack almost as much as eating it! You will need vanilla wafer cookies, canned vanilla frosting, chocolate covered mint patties, honey, sesame seeds, and shredded coconut (optional). Lightly frost the flat side of a vanilla wafer for the bottom "bun". Place a mint "burger" pattie on it. If desired, add green food coloring to the coconut, and place a little "lettuce" on the burger. Frost another vanilla wafer to secure the top bun. Brush the top of the cookie with a little warm honey and sprinkle on sesame seeds. Eat!

Walk on the Wild Side

Heading outside for a walk
can be a welcome change of pace
for a grandmother and the kids.
Combine a scavenger hunt with
your neighborhood saunter. Give
your grandchildren a list of items
they need to find along the way,
such as a bird, 3 kinds of flowers,
a bug, a barking dog,
a motorcycle, a police car,
10 mailboxes, etc. Have them
work together as a team to try to
check everything off the list.

Lipstick Races

Several tubes of lipstick, a flight of stairs, and a towel or blanket is all you need for your grandchildren to host a race unlike any other! Lay a towel or blanket "racetrack" on a staircase. Have one grandchild sit at the top of the stairs and another sit at the bottom. Set the lipstick tubes on the top step, on top of the blanket. When you say GO, each grandchild pulls the end of the "racetrack" taut, setting the lipsticks rolling downhill toward the finish line. Guess which "shade" will be the fastest!

Fireworks and Floral Art

Your grandchildren can paint eye-catching fireworks or flower bouquets easily, just by trading a cardboard tube for a paintbrush. Cut slits up one end of an empty toilet paper tube, leaving at least 2" of the top intact. Vary the length and width of the cut "flaps" on different tubes. Pour washable poster paint into paper plates, separated by color. Holding the uncut edge of the tube, have your grandchildren push the tube down into the paint, which will spread the cut flaps outward. (Use a different tube for each different color.) Have your grandchildren place the paint-edged tube, pushing down gently, on a large piece of cardboard or poster paper. Repeat, layering different colors. Try this on a grander scale by using paper towel tubes! (Be sure to cover all work surfaces, floors, and clothing, or better yet, do this outside on a calm day.)

Busy Bag Puppets

Before you set out on a car trip,
have grandkids color paper
sandwich bags as people or animals.
Fold the bottom of the bag over to
make the mouth, and have kids add
ears, nose, eyes, and hair
with crayons, or bits of fabric or
construction paper. Kids can chatter
away with their puppets for miles!

What's In My Purse?

When you're out and about, something that's always close at hand is your purse. If you're facing an unexpectedly long wait, why not use it to keep your grandchildren entertained? Grab one small item from your purse. Hiding it in your hand, hand it off to one of your grandchildren, keeping the item hidden. If your grandchild has any questions about what it is, allow them to whisper their questions in your ear. Then have the other grandkids try to guess what the secret item is by asking questions such as, "Does it make a sound?" "Can you use it to buy things?" or "Can you wear it?"

Center Stage

Kids love being the center
of attention. Give your
grandchildren this opportunity
by helping them make their own
family music video. Encourage
them to work together to choose
a favorite song. Then, turn up
the volume! On your phone,
record their antics as they
dance and sing to the music.
Depending on their age and
interest, help them dress up
in costume or work on
choreography before filming.
Their efforts may become
a family classic!

Delicious Log Cabin

Let your grandkids become the architect of their own snack time. Set out pretzel sticks, peanut butter, and graham crackers. (You may want to keep some moistened handwipes nearby. This is going to get sticky!) Help your grandchildren spread peanut butter on top of the graham cracker squares. Then, add more peanut butter on the side of each graham rectangle or square to "glue" it into a house shape. Push pretzel "logs" onto the walls and roof of the cabin, biting off the ends of the pretzels to fit. When the cabin is complete, it's snack time!

This or That?

Get to know each other better—
anytime, anywhere—with an
impromptu round of "This or
That?" Take turns asking each to
choose their favorite between two
related things, such as "Winter
or summer?" "Sweet or salty?"
"Beach or mountains?" "Math
or spelling?" "Dogs or cats?"
It's a fun way to pass the time,
while you learn more about your
grandchildren's preferences.

Shoebox Shenanigans

Repurpose old shoeboxes (or any cardboard box you have on hand) into kid-friendly creations. Depending on the age and interest of your grandchildren, help them fashion shoeboxes into racing cars, stuffed animal habitats, dinosaur dioramas, doll houses, or treasure boxes. Challenge them to come up with a list of all the wonderful ways they can think of to use an old box in a new way.

Picnic Basket Pastime

Here's a memory game you can play anywhere. Begin by saying, "In my picnic basket I packed..." Then name an item. The next player has to repeat the phrase, "In my picnic basket I packed..." repeating your item and adding a new item of his or her choice. This continues with everyone taking turns, repeating the list and adding a new item, until someone forgets something that's been packed for the picnic!

No Mess Masterpiece

If your grandchildren love to paint, but you're hesitant to encourage their creative efforts because of the potential mess it can make, here's an easy grandma hack: use a large, clean, plastic container set on its side as a canvas. Have grandkids paint the bottom of the container with washable paints. Use what's now the floor of the container as a palette, where the budding artists can mix their paints. Set a small plastic bowl of water in the corner of the larger container, so your grandkids can clean their brush, as needed. When it's time to begin another masterpiece, simply wash the paint off the plastic and start again. But, take a photo first!

Up and Down Cups

Challenge your grandchildren to
see how high of a tower they can
build from plastic or disposable
cups. Then, give them a clean,
balled up sock and have them
knock it down. Repeat!

Listen Carefully

When it's time to quiet down, here's an easy game to help your grandchildren stop and listen. Gather several items from around your home that you can use to make sounds. Then, have your grandchildren sit quietly with their eyes closed. You can tie bandanas over their eyes, if they're prone to peeking. Make different sounds and have your grandkids guess what item you're using. For instance, run your fingers along the edge of a comb, turn on a blow dryer, click a ballpoint pen, open a DVD case, crumple a piece of paper, sweep a broom across the kitchen floor, lock the sliding glass door, etc.

Brain Teaser

In this classic memory game, you place a number of different objects on a tray and allow players to study the assortment for about 30 seconds. Then you take the tray away and see how many objects players can recall. But there is no reason why you can't take this game on the road! Display a handful of objects from your purse or objects that are already on the table at a restaurant. After 30 seconds, put the objects back in your purse or move what's on the table into your lap. See how many objects your grandchildren can name from memory.

Photo Fun

If you're like most grandmothers, you have at least one box of old photographs stored away, waiting until you have time to scan them, put them into an album, or do anything other than allow them to collect dust. This is a perfect project to tackle with your grandchildren's help. First, sort out the rejects together. Invite your grandkids to choose a photo and write a journal entry or story about it. Let them use the rest to make a collage or glue individual faces on cardboard toilet paper tubes to make "family" totem poles. Sort the "keepers" into piles, sharing stories as you work. Have your grandchildren help scan the photos (after all, working with a phone or computer is often their forte!) or work with you to place them in albums.

Carpet Gymnastics

Sometimes, grandkids just need to burn off a little energy. However, it can be tough to find enough space to allow a little roughhousing inside. Here's a way to contain the chaos, while challenging them with a focused physical activity. Put two parallel lines of masking tape on the carpet of your largest room, 4" apart. This will serve as a "balance beam." Make it as long as space allows. Then, have your grandchildren try out different moves without "falling off." Have them take turns trying to jump, spin, or try forward and backward rolls. Then, have them make a set routine and compete against each other.

Light Flight

When the sun goes down, a flashlight is all you need for some nighttime fun. Turn off all of the lights and sweep a flashlight beam around the room. Have the grandkids see how long they can stay out of the light. Or try Flashlight Freeze, where your grandkids dance to the music until you shine a light on them and then they have to freeze in place. Play Hide and Seek, using only a flashlight. Have a contest to see who can make the funniest, or scariest, face by putting the flashlight below their chin. And remember, reading a book by flashlight in a fort made of blankets is always a great way to spend an evening at grandma's house.

Cheese Ball Critters

Cheese balls may be a traditional treat, but here's an unconventional way to enjoy them with your grandkids. Beat together 8 oz. of cream cheese, ½ C butter, and ¼ tsp. vanilla. Add ¾ C confectioner's sugar, 2 Tbsp. brown sugar, and ¾ C miniature chocolate chips. Make sure your grandchildren's hands are CLEAN and dry. Then, spray their hands with nonstick cooking spray. Give each child a portion of the cheese mixture to fashion into an animal shape. Have them cover their animal with crushed cookie or cracker crumbs (try chocolate wafer cookies, gingersnaps, saltines, or goldfish crackers). Decorate with nuts, raisins, or small candies. Refrigerate for 2 hours. Serve with pretzel sticks and graham crackers.

Character Study

Here's another easy guessing game to play on the go. Have your grandchildren take turns thinking of a character from a movie. Following the "20 Questions" format, everyone takes a turn asking the "character" questions about him or herself, such as, "Do you have super-powers?" "Do you sing?" "Are you an animal?" "Are you a princess?"

Bridge Building Competition

With a package of disposable straws and a dispenser of scotch tape, your grandchildren have all they need to become bridge builders. Make their project more challenging by asking them to build a bridge between two objects that is sturdy enough to roll a small ball across or support 100 pennies. When their bridge is complete, they may even want to build a straw city surrounding it.

Spider Web Toss

Help your grandchildren build a
spider's web with painter's tape
across a doorway, sticky side out.
Put another small piece of tape on
the carpet to mark the "throw" line.
Then, have your grandchildren
tear pages from an old magazine,
crumpling each page into a ball.
The goal is to toss the "ball" gently
enough so that it sticks to the tape
web without falling to the ground.

Penny Pitcher

Give each of your grandchildren 10 small pieces of foil and have them crumble into balls. Put a piece of tape on the floor to mark the line they kneel behind to try tossing their foil balls. (Masking tape works best on carpet and painter's tape works best on hard surfaces.) Stick three more pieces of tape on the floor, marking different distances between the starting line and the wall. On the one closest to the wall write 20. On the one in the middle write 10. On the one closest to the starting line write 5. Grandkids have to bounce the foil balls off of the wall. If their foil ball lands between the wall and closest piece of tape to it, they receive 20 points. If it lands between the first piece of tape and the middle piece, they receive 10 points, etc. See who can get to 100 points first!

Potato People

Cut the top off of a potato. Help your grandchildren hollow out the inside with a melon baller, going about ½ way down and leaving ½″ outer shell all the way around. Then, have them make faces on the potato by gluing on add-on pieces or drawing on features with felt pens. Use toothpicks to make "legs" that will hold the potato person upright. Place a moist cotton ball inside each potato and sprinkle the top of the cotton ball with birdseed. If your grandchildren are only with you for the afternoon, have them take their potato people home. If they gently water the inside of their potato twice a week, in a few weeks their potato person will grow its own hair.

Chopstick Relay

Mastering the art of using chopsticks is not only good for a child's (or grand-mother's!) manual dexterity, it can also make eating a meal a lot of fun. But chopsticks are not only suitable for eating Asian take-out. Use them for a relay race that requires concentration and fine motor skills. Give each child a small bowl of assorted items, such as dried pasta, dried beans, nuts, sunflower seeds, or hard candies, and an empty plastic cup. Using only chopsticks, your grandchildren compete to see who can get all of the items out of their bowl and into their cup the fastest. If they drop an item on the table, they have to put it back into their bowl and try again. No fingers allowed!

Bubble Battle

Blowing bubbles can be considered "kid stuff" by the 8 to 12-year old crowd. But turn bubble blowing into a competition—and suddenly it's cool again. Hang a hula-hoop and have your grandkids try to blow bubbles through it. See who can produce the most bubbles in one blow. Play bubble tag using bubbles to touch each other instead of hands. Blow bubbles off a balcony and see how far they can fly. Invite your grandchildren to come up with their own competitive events! If you don't have bubble solution on hand, here's an easy recipe: 3 C water, 1/2 C of light corn syrup, 1 C clear dishwashing liquid.

Even Bigger Bubbles!

Where grandkids are concerned, bigger is usually better! Hold a Biggest Bubble competition! Make Big Bubble wands with two straws and about 6 feet of yarn. (Try different lengths of yarn to vary the size of the bubbles.) Thread the yarn through the straws and tie a knot to secure. Have your grandchildren hold a straw in each hand and dip their bubble wand into a shallow, casserole-sized dish of bubble solution. Keeping the tips together, lift out and gently spread the straws apart as you walk backwards stretching the wand to its full size.

Hint: cloudy or overcast days are best for blowing bubbles! Direct sunshine, low humidity, or a little bit of wind can dry out your bubbles and make them pop more quickly.

I See...

Whether you're relaxing out on the patio, or stuck in line at the bank, here's a game you can play that is guaranteed to help you and your grandchildren see more than you did at first glance. Take turns saying, "I see..." and then listing one thing you can see from where you are standing or sitting. The more obscure you get, the more fun it is to play!

*I see...
an animal home*

Photo Globes

   Photos don't all need to be framed to be displayed! Gather photos of your grandchildren, printing copies from images on your computer or using small-sized school photos or snapshots. Give each grandchild a small, clean, glass jar. Cut the person out of the photo, cutting away any background images. Cover the photo, front and back, with clear, heavy-duty, packing tape. Cut around the edges to create the desired shape. Tape the image onto the inside of the lid, using a small piece of packing tape on both sides, securing the image in an upright position. Fill the jar with light corn syrup or baby oil, adding glitter, sparkles, sequins, or plastic "jewels," as desired. Tightly secure the lid, give the snow globe a good shake, and set it upside down to display.

Grandma's Book Club

Spending time in the company of good books is a habit that provides lifelong benefits. Help foster your grandchildren's literary love with a little incentive program. Give them each a sheet of paper, or better yet, their own "reader's" journal, to keep a list of all the books they read. Set up goals for each grandchild, depending on age and reading proficiency. Give each grandchild a reward for each level they achieve (such as reading at least one book a week, or for every ten books they read, or for reading a book that is longer than 50 pages, etc.) If your grandchildren, don't live near you, have them bring a list of books they've read since their last visit, signed by their parents, to include in their challenge.

Instant Race Track

If your grandchildren are fans of cars, trucks, and anything else that happens to have wheels, build them a roaming race track on your patio, around your garage, or throughout several rooms of your home. Using masking or painter's tape, weave a set of parallel lines as far as you you care to go. Get creative. Set the track to run up the side of a footstool or over a stack of books, into and out of the tub, up a flight of stairs, etc. No need for rules. Just let your grandkids enjoy racing their own cars around the track. If they didn't bring any toys with them, no problem. Racing imaginary cars can be just as much fun! Get creative and use household items like a spool of thread on its side or empty plastic bottle.

Rainy Day Sorbet

Any season is the right time to enjoy a tart sorbet. All you need is 1 lb. of fresh strawberries, 1 C sugar, ½ C water, ¼ C lemon juice, and ¼ tsp. salt. Have your grandchildren pull the stems off of the strawberries. Cut each one in half. If using fresh citrus, juice the lemons. Mix the lemon juice, sugar, water, and salt, and bring the mixture to a boil over medium heat. Take the mixture off of the heat and let it cool. Pour the cooled syrup into a blender. Add the strawberries, blending until smooth. Pour the mixture into a shallow, freezable container. Stir the mixture every 30 minutes, until it is smooth. When it reaches the desired frozen consistency, eat! Once you've perfected strawberry, experiment with different types of fresh fruit and flavorings.

Strike Up the Band

You don't need traditional instruments to make beautiful music together. Choose a simple familiar tune. Then, challenge your grandchildren to play it with something they can find in your house. Have them brainstorm what they could use as instruments. If they need help getting started, suggest blowing across the top of a bottle, hitting different sized pans with a wooden spoon, clinking drinking glasses gently with chopsticks, hold a piece of paper against a comb and humming, shaking a box of pasta or rice, stepping on a squeaky stair, or even flushing the toilet! Challenge them to see how many different instruments they can create. Then, have them perform their tune!

Milk Jug Juggle

If you have a couple of empty
plastic milk jugs, you have what
you need for a fun-filled game of
skill. Cut the bottom off of the
clean milk jug, leaving the handle
intact. Discard the bottom of the
jug in recycling. Cover the cut edge
of the top of the jug with duct tape
to make it smooth and safe. Then,
give your grandkids balled socks,
or crumpled balls of paper or foil,
and challenge them to toss the
objects back and forth,
moving farther away from each
other the better they get.

Jug-O'-Lanterns

Whether you use them at Halloween to make pumpkin-free Jack-o'-lanterns, or year-round to display your grandchildren's artwork, plastic milk jugs are the easy way to light up the night with fun. Take a clean gallon jug, and Grandma, you do this step: cut a hole, about 1½" in diameter, near the bottom. Have your grandchildren decorate the outside of the jugs with waterproof permanent markers. Then, put a string of Christmas lights inside the jug, with the plug extending outside from the hole in the back. Set up outdoors near an outlet. After the sun sets, light up your porch with your grandchildren's artwork.

Spell It Out

Here's a great way to help your grandchildren practice their spelling while having fun as they do it. First, choose a category that suits their age group, such as animals, food, or states. The first person chooses the word. The next person has to say the first letter. Everyone takes turns spelling out the word, one person saying one letter at a time. The person who says the final letter immediately shouts DONE! Then, he or she gets to choose the next word. If someone misspells the word along the way, allow them to try again until they get it right. If it's a young child, the others can give a hint, like posing in the shape of the letter, or forming it with their fingers.

Big or Small, Celebrate It All

It doesn't take much to turn what would otherwise be an ordinary day into a special celebration. If your grandchildren have accomplished something noteworthy, such as making the softball team, getting an A on a spelling test, or even speaking nicely to their sibling the entire time they were at your house, go out of your way to let them know their efforts haven't gone unnoticed. Or simply celebrate the fact that you are blessed to have them as your grandkids! Add candles to that peanut butter and jelly sandwich. Attach streamers to the chair of whoever could use a little extra hoopla. Wrap up a small gift—just because—and place it on their pillow. After all, everyone needs to be reminded that they're loved, appreciated, and worthy of celebration!

Don't Say It!

Here's a game you can play all day, regardless of what else is on the agenda. Choose a word that you will all be forbidden to say that day. Try: why, when, how, me, you, or I. Then set a cup or jar out for each person— including you. Every time someone says the forbidden word, they receive a token in their cup. (You can use paper- clips, checkers, dried beans...whatever is handy.) Whoever has the fewest tokens in their cup at the end of the day is crowned the Word Wizard. You can decide what reward that honor deserves!

Huff and Puff

See how long your grandchildren can keep
a cotton ball aloft with this simple game.
Cut a circle out of a sheet of paper. Make
one slit, stopping about ¾ of the way to
the center. Overlap the edges, making
a cone shape and tape into place. Cut
a small hole in the center of the circle,
large enough to fit a bendable straw. With
the inside of the cone pointing upwards,
insert the long end of the straw from the
bottom, so that it extends about 1½".
Secure the paper cone to the straw. Make
sure there are no air holes around it.
Then, have your grandchildren
hold a cotton ball,
ping pong ball, or ball
of paper or foil,
over the opening in
the cone and blow.

Fun with Your Family Tree

Help your grandchildren gain a better sense of where they fit into your family by creating a family tree together. Gather old photos of family members. Scan and print family photos, or use the photos that were never quite good enough to make it into the family album! Draw a family graph, listing relatives' names and birthdates as far back as you can. Attach photos when possible. Invite your grandchildren to draw in any likenesses that are missing. Then, have them draw a tree around the graph. Talk about every person on the tree, sharing as many stories as possible. Encourage lots of questions!